Williams

Track

By

Joel Richardson

Table of Contents

Chapter 1 – The Plansky and Farley Years

Chapter 2 – 1988-2001

Chapter 3 – 2002-present

Prologue

This book is an attempt to capture the competitiveness, spirit, and search for excellence of the Williams track team, as well as the, at times, somewhat less serious side of the team. The book is not an attempt to be encyclopedic in either spirit or fact, and covers neither every highlight of competition, nor every side of the Williams track personality. What it does try to do is give a notion of what Williams track is all about, since my belief is that it is one of the greatest things about a Williams experience.

Some of the people I interviewed for the book asked me why I was doing it. It's not for money, because I have no idea what the sales will be for this book, but I wrote a book about my high school team and enjoyed the process of meeting all the former athletes and finding out about the history and some of the stories. I thought the same thing would happen with a book about my college team, and it turned out it did. I hope you enjoy reading it as much as I enjoyed writing it.

Tony Plansky

The Plansky and Farley Years

Williams track has a long and storied history, both competitively and philosophically. The first record of competition was in 1874 when a meet was held pitting Ephs against each other. Events contested included pole vaulting, standing jump, high kick, half mile, putting light weight, running long jump, throwing base ball, Siamese twin race, three-legged race, half-mile scrub race, and mile, which was won by Wilder, '77, in 5:21.

Moving ahead to 1935, the program was taken over by new head coach Tony Plansky. Plansky was a tremendous all-around athlete who was voted second best American athlete of the first half of the 20th century behind Jim Thorpe. A graduate of Georgetown University, he was the varsity fullback on the football team, and also captured the National AAU Decathlon championship. At 6'2" and 220 lbs., he ran a 10 flat 100 yards, put the shot 49', and long jumped 23'6". He played for the New York Giants of the NFL as well as minor league baseball. However, once he assumed his coaching position at Williams, he retired from competitive sports, apart from an occasional low 70's round of golf. By all accounts he was a true gentleman and sportsman, believing along with the prevailing ethos of the time, that it was not whether you won or lost, but how you played the game that counted. Plansky was presented with a special coach's award at the IC4A indoor games at Madison Square Garden, citing him for his "outstanding adherence to the principles of good sportsmanship."

One of the track stars of the late 40's and early 50's was Kevin Delany. Kevin ran the mile, 1000, 880, and 4 x 440. He was a veteran of the Navy and attended on the GI Bill. The campus was a culture shock to the Brooklyn native who says "track was my entry point to college and helped me fit in." Plansky was a father figure who told him, "Delany you can't run fast enough to keep warm," referring to the flow of blood generated by physical exertion.

Outdoor Board Track

The winter team trained on an outdoor board track and he reports, "We didn't bust our butts the way people are expected to do today." In 1949 he broke F I Newton's 1911 mile school record of 4:26 with a 4:20 clocking, and also captured the 880 mark with a 1:57. As a post-grad he finished 6th in the AAU with a 4:13 at a time when the world record was 4:01.4 by Gunder Haag of Sweden. He later snagged the mark in the 1000 at 2:14.5..

WILLIAMS TRACK and FIELD RECORDS

Event	Record	Holder	Date	Event	Record	Holder	Date
100 Yard	9.7	Bob Schumo	May 6 39				
220 Yard	21.4	C.W. Miller	May 2 31	Mile Relay	3.22.2	J.W. Veitor	41
440 Yard	49.4	C.H. Stovers	May 19 25	"	"	P.S. Parish	
880 Yard	1.57	X.J. Delany	May 17 49	"	"	W.A. Peck	
1 Mile	4.20.7	X.J. Delany	April 30 49	"	"	J.D. VanCott	
2 Mile	9.27.6	H.H. Brown	May 29 20	Two Mile Relay	8.04.5	W.R. Barney	49
120 Yard high hurdle	15.1	R.W. Moore	May 15 38	"	"	W.E. Ziegenhals	
220 Yard low hurdle	24.2	R.W. Moore	May 15 38	"	"	G.L. Smith	
Shot Put	47'5"	R.E. Lamberton	April 27 35	"	"	X.J. Delany	
Hammer Throw	155'10.5"	O.Z. Wood	May 18 40	Pole Vault	12.7 3/4	Kenneth Perry	May 16 53
Discus Throw	138'9"	W.Ed. Bauer	April 30 32	220 Yard	21.3	Robert Y. Behr	May 28 54
Javelin Throw	180'3"	D. Dunn	May 11 40	Discus Throw	151'1¼"	Edward D. Reeves	May 6 55
Broad Jump	23'7"	X.X. Flint	May 15 33	Hammer	163'8¾"	Edward D. Reeves	May 27 55
High Jump	6'2.5"	S.X. Urner	May 15 33	High Jump	6'3⅝"	C.A. Schweighauser	May 26 56
Pole Vault	12'2.5"	E.E. Dissell	May 25 31				
Cross Country	20.37	W. Kelton	Oct 22 48				

The team's schedule at the time consisted of 4-5 dual meets with schools such as Middlebury, Union, RPI, and Little 3 rivals Amherst and Wesleyan. They would also run the 4x440 at the Millrose Games and Boston Garden. One of Delany's teammates was Lionel Bolin, grandson of Gaius Bolin, who was one of the first two people of color to attend Williams. At Lionel's time there were only two other African-Americans on campus. He reports receiving bad vibes from one tennis coach, but other than that there were no troubles.

He remembers Tony Plansky for the attitude he had, of not taking it too seriously, not a world-shaking event. He ran mostly the 440. While Plansky wanted him to try the 880, he declined.

Indoor Track at Williams

Bob Behr reports the beginning of the Southern Spring Break trip in 1955. Perhaps envious of the baseball and golf teams, a carload had traveled to the University of Miami in 1954, but the next year a larger team went south with scrimmages against Davidson, Virginia Tech, and Richmond. The meets were set up by Behr with an assist going to Harvard's captain Bob Rittenburg, later an Olympic team alternate. While the meet at Davidson was rained out, VPI offered some good workouts and finally Richmond offered some strong competition. Plansky did not accompany the team.

For the sake of comparison, the outdoor school records as of April 2, 1968 were as follows:

100 – 9.7, Robert Schumo, May 6, 1939.

220 -21.0, Dick Horner, April 23, 1966.

440 – 48.2, George Sudduth, May 30, 1958.

880 -1:53.6. Roger Maynard, May 13, 1967.

Mile – 4:16.7, Steve Orr, May 14, 1966.

Two Mile – 9:27.6, H.H. Brown, May 29, 1920.

440 Relay – 43.2 – Browne, Dewart, Scarola, Maynard, May 14, 1965.

Mile Relay – 3:20.8 – Horner, Dewart, Scarola, Maynard, May 13, 1967.

120 HH – 15.1 – Roger Moore, May 13, 1938.

440 IH – 57.0, Doug Rae, May 14, 1966.

Shot Put – 47'7 ½", Bill Hufnagel, May 11, 1962.

Pole Vault – 13'1 ¼", Bill Gardner, May 21, 1966.

Discus – 151' 1 ½", Ned Reeves, May 27, 1955.

Long Jump – 23' 7", Bradford Flint, May 12, 1923.

Javelin – 192' 4 ½", Bob Hatcher, May 17, 1958.

Hammer – 163' 8 ½", Ned Reeves.

High Jump – 6' 3 5/8", Charley Schweighauser, May 26, 1956.

Triple Jump – 45' 1 ½", Tom Chapman, May 21, 1966.

The early '70's saw a trio of distance stars in Jay Haug, Pete Farwell, and Tom Cleaver. Haug would go on to hold 16 school records at graduation. His marks included a 4:12 mile, 9:01 deuce and 14:09 three mile. Haug reports his later inspiration came from viewing the movie, "Chariots of Fire". He still runs today and ran a 30 minute 10K post grad and also won the 1982 Foxtrotter Marathon in 2:24:12. Track was extremely important to him with his best friends coming from the team and Christian Fellowship. Haug believes Williams has a good niche, attracting the good athlete who will not compete professionally but still believes sports are important. Haug was awarded the Purple Key Trophy to the athlete who best exemplifies leadership, team spirit, ability and character.

73 Indoor Team

Tom Cleaver ran mostly the mile and three mile, his best time was a 4:17 indoors at Colby. He believes that track undoubtedly helped with his education, the teammates were very, very close and it was a large part of his Williams experience, with incredible personalities. "Tony Plansky was an unbelievable guy in terms of demeanor and it was hard to put into words what he gave to the team. " He reports he is in awe of what has happened with the team becoming a Division III national power in the past twenty years. "It appears to me that (Peter) Farwell had everything to do with the team's success." "It was a really fun time, we ran (the Boston Marathon) as freshmen, it was a three hour release from academics. The other guys got you through practice; we started to see each other outside of track. It was a huge part of my experience and enhanced it to a great deal."

The first ever indoor track meet at Williams was staged at the Herbert Towne Field House in January of 1972. Union College won the meet with Williams second and Hamilton third. Notable was Williams freshman Pete Mertz winning the high jump in a new school record 6' 6 ½ ".

Indoor school records as of 1973 were as follows:

Shot Put – Lester - 50' 1 ½" Feb. 5, 1972.

Long Jump – Brady - 22' 5 ½" March 14, 1957.

Pole Vault – Burns – 13' 3 ½" Feb. 2, 1973.

High Jump – Mertz – 6' 6 ½ "Feb. 5, 1972.

60 – Newsome – 6.2 – Feb. 16, 1973.

60 HH – Reed – 7.4 – Feb. 12, 1972.

600 – Sheils – 1:14.6 – Feb .16, 1973.

1000 – Delany – 2:14.8 – March 17, 1950.

Mile – Haug – 4:12.9 – Jan. 27, 1973.

2 Mile – Haug – 9:01.8 – Feb. 10, 1973.

Mile Relay – Newsome, Sheils, Parker, Reed, 3:22.4, Feb. 24, 1973.

2 Mile Relay – Cleaver, Holman, Haug, Huntington, 7:57.5, Feb. 14, 1971

Distance Medley – Hyde, Reed, Cleaver, Haug, 10:25.6, Jan. 6, 1973.

In 1974 junior hurdler Mike Reed was ablaze. He finished sixth at the IC4A's in the 440 intermediate hurdles in a time of 52.2, and followed that up with a 14.5 second victory in the 120 Highs at the New England Championships at Brown. At the Easterns Reed would win the high hurdles and finish fifth in the intermediates despite hitting the last hurdle. Meanwhile, Co-captain Jeff Elliot would win the 440 in 50.5.

In 1976 Scott Perry would win the indoor Easterns Long Jump at 24' ¼". Perry was an enormously talented athlete who could compete and win a variety of sprints, jumps

Lee Jackson
Capt 79

and relays and would go on to star in the NFL.

79 Indoor

Calvin Schnure '81 is still the school record holder for the indoor 500 meters (He actually ran 600 yards but the time is converted). He felt it was easier to compete because there were so many events indoors, and attributes his record's longevity to the fact that the event is rarely run. He ran only indoors as a freshman and sophomore, doing crew in the spring. The team's New England Division III championship in the 4 x 440 convinced him to go out for spring track, though he liked crew as well. The most important lesson for Schnure was working with Coach Farley as a role model and trying to do the right thing. He enjoyed track as an outlet from book learning and attributes the recent success of the track team to "success breeds success". When he was there teams (relays) could not go to nationals, though individuals could but he was not bitter about that. He believes the priorities were in the right place. Calvin ran at the nationals in the 800 in a heat including MIT's Paul Neves. He took the pace out at a fast rate and though he did not qualify for the final, takes pride in pushing the pace and "not letting someone walk away with an easy win."

Steve (Bat) Bellerose '82 competed in the 400, 600, and 800 and acquired the nickname "Two Flat Bat" for his consistency at turning the two laps of the outdoor track in exactly two

Coach Dick Farley

minutes. Bellerose recalls visiting the school and being surprised by the outdoor track, (the old three laps to a mile, square cinders) and finding it much worse than his high school facility. He also found there was a marked difference in the level of training in college and was frequently found recovering from his indoor workouts outside of the field house in the cold.

Steve respected Coach Farley and considers himself lucky to have had him as a coach. He believes Farley had the right work-life balance as his young (at the time) children were frequently running around the practice field. Farley also watched Steve win the Alumni Mile at his 15th year college reunion and congratulated the winner, "Christ Bellerose that's better than you ever ran while you were here!" Bellerose went on to triathlons and marathons but had to stop running due to a back injury, though he still cycles and swims and considers exercise "absolutely a great stress relief".

The legendary Dick Farley was head track coach in the 70's and 80's until he began his National Hall of Fame career running the football program. A colorful figure known for his outrageous wardrobe, Farley notes how much times have changed in the track program from his time. "Everything is a time trial, there are no dual or tri meets, the athletes are just trying to qualify for the championship meets." He believes the best meet of the year is the Division I New Englands, rather than the Nationals, because it includes more of the team while maintaining a high level of competition. He also agrees with Pete Farwell that the Division I and III New Englands are better than earlier meets because for the first time in the season the athletes will bond with one another, as they are looking to a team score and one person's performance affects another's.

Another difference is the depth of the coaching staff. While currently there are five to six people, in his time he had one or two assistants at most. The present day team has reduced numbers, so some athletes who try out do not make the squad. There is now a Club Track team, organized by students, that trains on their own and competes in some meets and road races. :Farley's coaching style is the same he learned at Boston University running with Olympic Gold Medalist David Hemery: run hard one day, easy the next. He also will do some aquatic work in the pool and notes a philosophical similarity with Head Cross Country and Assistant Track Coach Pete Farwell. Farley values hard work and notes that while football was always a matter of either winning or losing, with track the goal was for an athlete to reach their full potential, regardless of position. "Try to reach your full potential whatever that might be," and "you need to coach when things don't go well," which means you learn more about yourself when losing than winning.

Finally, a couple of anecdotes: At one point the Williams team was facing Amherst and looked on paper to lose by 40 points. The athletes at practice were a little less than serious and Farley, ever the pessimist, informed them "If you beat Amherst I'll kiss your (rear) at high noon on Spring Street." Sure enough the team pulled off the upset and Farley, not wanting to renege, made good on his promise, while noting he "kissed their underwear."

The other story was when three or four of his distance crew threatened to run the Boston Marathon in spring and skip outdoor track. In typical fashion Farley informed them that it takes no talent to complete a marathon, that anyone could do it. They told him if he ran the marathon they would run spring track, and so run the marathon he did, in 3:45, a respectable time for a muscular man in the heat.

Peter Farwell
74 Boston Marathon

1988-2001

When Farley stepped down to take the football job in the late 80's, the reins were ceded to Pete Farwell, who became head coach of Cross Country, Indoor, and Outdoor track. Farwell was a Williams alum from Illinois who qualified for the Olympic Trials in the marathon. Entering his 30th season as XC head, he notes that since 1912 there have been only three men at the helm, first Doc Seely, then Tony Plansky, and then Pete.

Farwell believes currently there is too much emphasis on the nationals, which involve only the elite of the team and leaves out the majority. In a theme that recurred throughout the research of this book, he believes there needs to be a balance between team and individual goals. The process of developing as an athlete is more important than actually achieving a particular mark or performance. Division III New Englands are a highlight because more athletes can compete and score, whether in an individual event or relay. Pete enjoys coaching when the whole team is involved, recalling a dual meet with MIT when the outcome came down to the final event being contested, which was the pole vault. Members of both teams were crowded around the standards, cheering. He does not consciously teach job-skill related values, but teamwork, having fun, and cultural values. He counsels any athlete who needs it and recalls his favorite classes while pursuing his Master's were the counseling electives.

He believes it is important to listen to people, that athletes like to know you as a person. Occasionally he will hear from an athlete or parent sometime after the fact, what a pleasure it was to stop for a picnic on the way home from a meet, or letting lesser athletes still compete. All have equal time in practice, and they can fill different roles on the team, such as social organizer, coach's helper, cheerleader, etc.

He encourages athletes to work out in the offseason, whether it be weights or running. NCAA regulations prohibit off season coaching between coaches and athletes, but suggestions can be made ahead of time. He suggests they work on form and cadence while trying to keep up their stride ratio at the same time as maintaining stride length, to make for a faster run. He also advises striding so the foot lands below the body to increase firing power.

He respects Tony Plansky as having been casual and well-rounded while not super competitive. "Being a coach is a good life – it's meaningful – (you) make a difference in a person's life." On winning the Director's Cup annually, an award given to the Division III School with the best national sports programs, Farwell notes," People really respect Williams because we win the Director's Cup in such a good way, and can perform academically at the same time."

The 1992 Men's Outdoor team captured both the NESCAC and Div. III New England Championships. The star at NESCAC's was Larry Smith, who set a conference record in winning the 400 in 48.77, also captured the 200 in 21.99, and anchored the 4x100 and 4x400 relays. Other blue ribbons went to Jonathan Lindley in the 100 (11.0), Ethan Brooks in the shot (45'9"), Todd Ducharme in the high jump (6'7"), Keith Long in the 800 (1:58.22), Chad Kurtz in the 1500 (3:58.6), and Brian Coan in the 10K (31:56).

The Division III New Englands were held at Tufts University in Medford MA. The Ephs won by over 50 points, with 122 to runner up Coast Guard's 70. The six first places came from Coan in the 10K (32:08), Kurtz in the 1500 (again 3:58.6), Smith in the 400 (48.93), Sal Salamone in the 400 hurdles (54.13), and Brooks in the shot put (48'5"), as well as the 4x100 relay. The women were second at Waterville Maine, with senior Cherie Macauley winning the 1500 at 4:41.38, Rebecca Adams in he 5K, 18:03, Cathleen Miller capturing the heptathlon with 3,463 points, and the 4x400 relay. At the Division I New Englands, Larry Smith qualified for Nationals with a runner up 48.05 in the 400, Seth McClennen's 9:17.3, good for 5th in the steeplechase, also earned him a Nationals bid, and likewise Salamone's 52.40 in the 400 hurdles, good for third place.

The 1993 women's indoor team captured the New England Division III Championship, edging out Tufts by four points. The team accounted for five blue ribbons. Captain Lee Keichel copped the 400 in 59.7, Angela Garcia won the high jump at 5'5", Alix Hyde took the pentathlon with 2,758, Nancy Byrne grabbed the 1000 at 3:04.2, and the 4x800 team of Byrne, Kelleher, Goetzinger and Zindell also took top honors. Earlier at the Williams Invitational Junior Todd Ducharme established two new school records with a high jump of 6'9 ¾" and a pentathlon score of 3,513 points.

At the Men's Div III, Williams also emerged victorious behind a number of strong efforts. Senior Captain Seth McClennen led the way with a facility record 8:38.44 in the 3000, and came back one half hour later to run a 4:19 mile as anchor for the third place distance medley team. McClennen felt that the leadership opportunities given him as captain for three seasons allowed him to learn diplomacy with teammates and later his patients in his career as a cardiologist. Most of his Williams memories were of track, which taught him how to be a person. He felt he learned more from track than classes.

One other victory came from Salamone with a 1:06 500, while Ducharme jumped 6'9" for second and also grabbed fourth in the hurdles, with teammate Andre Burrell nabbing third. Other highlights included sophomore Bobby Walker qualifying for the Nationals with a weight toss of 62'10", good for third place, and Greg Crowther's 5000 in 15:27, good for fourth.

In an online interview, Crowther sings the praises of his Williams track experience. He believes it benefited him in at least four different ways. First, it was a great way to make new friends. Greg describes himself as somewhat slow at this process, so daily workouts with the same people were essential. Second, it served as an outlet for his competitive instincts. Track allowed him to channel his competitive nature into something where the pursuit of victory is healthy, or at least not detrimental to others. Third, it gave him a vivid and dramatic lesson in his ability to change himself. He references an article by Adam Gopnik on the late Kirk Varnedoe '67, who played football at Williams before becoming a giant in the art world. To paraphrase Varnedoe, football allowed you to transform from your original self, to become a better self. It was a magical transformation. "Track may be an even better sport than football for learning this lesson, since changes in performance are so easy to quantify," notes Crowther. "It's hard to experience this sort of transformation and not be changed by it." Finally, it allowed him a lasting appreciation of sport. "We took ourselves seriously and trained hard, yet never lost sight that there was more to life than winning races. I give Peter Farwell a lot of credit for promoting and extending the values of his predecessors: respect for tradition, respect for the environment, concern for one's teammates, and the simple joys of running through the wilderness. I still run because, fundamentally, I'm still a competitive person. But I still enjoy it as much as I do in part because of Pete."

At the ECAC's in Brunswick Maine, senior captain Derek "Vinnie" Catsam outclassed the triple jump field with a leap of 45'5". Catsam is "proudest of the team accomplishments in what is often mistakenly viewed as an individual sport. I always wanted us to win as a team. Fortunately, we usually did." "The experience of competing for Williams was a valuable experience simply because in and of itself it had merit. Sometimes we lose sight of the fact that sports are in and of themselves worthwhile in our zeal to draw larger conclusions about teamwork and dealing with adversity and working hard and all of the clichés about sports that are no less true for being clichés."

"I also want to say a few words about my coaches, especially Pete Farwell, Davie Sheppard, and Dick Farley. In various ways I was blessed to be around these men. Coaches tend to be larger than life figures, especially when you are younger, and while by college I had developed more than my share of cynicism, it was still useful for me to have these sorts of figures guiding my way….I have drawn many lessons from those who helped steer my way in college." Derek's single proudest moment "came in 1992 when at the end-of-year picnic I was voted captain of the 1992-1993 teams….The fact that my teammates voted for me meant a great deal. But it also struck me that at this great institution, with a long history of trying to balance that Olympian ideal of the complete person, I had become a part, however small, of that history. I just remember walking back to my room after the picnic with this feeling of contentment and pride and at the same time humility and gratitude."

On a lighter note, Derek reveals the source of his nickname (Vinnie). "We were in Boston for a meet. I do not remember which one. Coach Davie Sheppard decided he wanted Legal Seafood. And he decided that he was dragging a bunch of us along with him. Well, the problem with that was that for a couple of us who did not come from comfortable backgrounds, our paltry meal money was simply not going to cover much of a meal. So a teammate and I ended up getting something like the cup of clam chowder while others are ordering all kinds of meals. It was real sitcom potential stuff if you ignore the clear class ramifications that it probably tells us about Williams. And the teammate and I had fairly legendary reputations for being serious eaters, so it was sort of obvious that something was up. Fortunately, though, we turned it into a joke, and somehow the scenario came up that I was going to be forced back into the kitchen to scale fish and wash dishes to pay for my clam chowder. Coach Shep thought it was a hilarious image, and that I'd be supervised by a fat guy wearing a greasy white v-neck t-shirt. His name would be Vinnie. From that point on, I was Vinnie."

The "Slow Boys" were a distinctly Williams phenomenon. Bob Kane '88 reports, "We began in the spring of 1985 during a practice just before Little Three. Dan Blatt '85, Dave Sprague '88, Mac Hines '88, and I ('88) were standing hear the old bleachers near our then 1/3 of a mile cinder track when Ted Arrowsmith '88 ran by us with Jon Ellison '86 and yelled over, "We're the fast boys." We became the Slow Boys after that, with some ground rules: every member had to have come in last in a race at some point (but could never have dropped out of one), and every member had to run their best. We had T-shirts made at that place that used to be next to Goff's which read Slow Boys '85 on the front and Fashionably Late on the back (purple with gold letters) and kept that tradition going as we recruited new members over the years. Jim Simmonds '89 and Kevin "Pokey" Walter '90, who were entrusted with the lead baton (that's "lead" the metal, definitely not the verb "Lead") made a video in 1988 or 1989."

Jeremy Fox '95 reports,"By the time I arrived at Williams, the Slow Boys had morphed into an exclusively x-country phenomenon. I knew that they were originally a track phenomenon, formed around 1984 or so in joking counterpoint to a group of sprinters who called themselves the Fast Boys. I don't know when the Slow Boys morphed into an x-country phenomenon or if they've since morphed back".

"When I was at Williams the current Slow Boys would hold a meeting before the end-of-season dinner and choose the new Slow Boys from the freshman. At the dinner, the new Slow Boys were inducted by the King Slow Boy by being dubbed with a lead baton, the baton being a holdover from the track origins of the Slow Boys. I do remember that Slow Boyness wasn't defined in terms of pure lack of speed. Greg Crowther '95 was a team captain and top 7 on the 1994 national championship-winning x-country team, but remained a Slow Boy. Lack of a kick and slow-looking or awkward form were clear criteria for being named a Slow Boy. Greg was fast, but his utter lack of finishing kick and his penchant for falling on mountain descents were considered very Slow Boyish. In our day, a certain bookishness also seemed to characterize the Slow Boys, although that wasn't an "official" criterion and wasn't always the case. The original Slow Boys were said to have been slow in part because they partied heavily. Lack of success with members of the opposite sex was another unofficial Slow Boy characteristic, which carried through from the days of the hard-partying Slow Boys to the more bookish Slow Boys of my time.

"Other than the induction itself, the Slow Boys didn't really have any official activities or anything. We did have official t-shirts printed for the Slow Boys 10th anniversary, with the slogan "Passed, Present, and Future," a quite clever idea of Gerry Siarney '95 (the previous Slow Boy "slogan" was "Festina Lente", which loosely translates as "Make Haste Slowly"). The Slow Boys were just a kind of little ongoing joke, which would be laughed at anew if a Slow Boy happened to do something particularly Slow Boyish.

"Sunday mountain runs were always a chancy thing for Slow Boys, because we'd fall behind the main pack and so run the risk of getting lost. I remember Gerry Siarney '95 going down the wrong side of Prospect and having to run back through North Adams, which was a very Slow Boy thing to do. He didn't get back to town until the evening. And I and another Slow Boy (don't recall who it was) once fell so far behind on Taconic that we thought we were lost and started yelling for help as we were running. But we weren't actually lost and eventually Pete ran back up the trail to ask us what we were yelling about, because the only thing wrong was that we were really, really slow.

"After I graduated, the new King Slow Boy, Joel Mandelman, started the Slow Boy Whopper Mile, which all the Slow Boys (and anyone else who wanted to participate) ran. It consisted of running a lap, then stopping and eating a Whopper, repeated for a total of 4 laps and three Whoppers. A very Slow Boyish thing to do. Don't know if that tradition is still going".

"Overall, the thing I remember most isn't so much any specific incident, but the unspoken function that the Slow Boys served. The Slow Boys, and Pete's support of them, helped make the slow guys feel like part of the team, rather than an afterthought. And I even think their existence was important to Pete for reasons that went beyond making guys like me and Gerry feel at home. A lot of Pete's x-country coaching was oriented towards keeping x-country fun and preventing an overly-competitive, it's-only-fun-when-we-win vibe from developing. I think Pete liked the Slow Boys because, whatever they were about, they certainly *weren't* about winning anything. "

The 1994 men's team won their third straight Div. III New England title. Senior captain Todd Ducharme scored 26 points alone, winning the pentathlon with 3445 points and placing second in the hurdles (7.75) and high jump (6'6 ¼"). The 4x400 squad of Duff, Blecher, Iliff, and Woelful was victorious, while silver medals went to Chad Kurtz, Bobby Walker in the weight throw, Brent Wilson in the dash, and the distance medley relay crew of Billo, Pisano, Ma, and Clancy. Not to be overlooked, Greg Crowther captured the 5000 in 15:06.51. At the Nationals Walker saved his best for last with a weight throw of 57'9 ¼", a personal best by three feet and new school record, good for third place. The men's 4x400 of Duff, Blecher, Iliff, and Clarke also earned All-American status with a fifth place finish. Also in '94 New England Runner magazine announced Pete Farwell as 1993 New England Coach of the Year. Farwell was lauded for his consistency and dedication toward building a top-notch program.

Farwell would go one further in 1995, being named the National Division III Men's Track Coach of the Year, In the Fall, he had been named National Men's Cross Country Coach of the Year, his harriers having won the National Title. Two of Farwell's top track athletes were actually field athletes, Bobby Walker and Ethan Brooks, both weightmen. Of Walker, when 18 of his athletic peers were polled on which Williams athlete was most admired, he was the unanimous choice noted. Notable about Walker, beyond his numerous championships and All-Americans, was the fact that as a sophomore he was fourth after one round in the hammer competition, but returned to campus because of mandatory Junior Advisor training that weekend, then went back to Nationals to compete in the Finals. Walker placed his priority on learning skills to be a father figure. Brooks was a three sport All-American in football, indoor track, and outdoor track, drafted by the Atlanta Falcons of the NFL, and NCAA champion and Record Holder in the 35 lb. weight and also NCAA champion in the Hammer Throw.

In an interview Brooks talks about playing in the NFL, where he labored for nine seasons. He believes his track experience definitely helped with football, as it made him a more explosive athlete, as well as forcing him to use every muscle in his body to react, which is essential when tackling in football. The other thing was learning the footwork necessary in the throwing circle, which was helpful on the line of scrimmage.

Ethan's highlight was competing and practicing every day with the other throwers. He looked forward to the challenge every day of seeing who would throw farthest in practice. The other highlight was the 1995 team which, between the men's and women's teams, featured five All-Americans in the hammer, including Brooks, Walker, Consigli, Brenda Start, and Lisa Chadderdon.

He believes being on any team helps you grow as a person, especially track and field where you have males and females and more different backgrounds, walks of life, and different people. He roomed with distance runner Marzuki Stephens at one point and recalls him as an artsy kind of guy, but soon found they had a lot in common and were not that different.

When applying to colleges he looked at some Division 1 schools but chose Williams because he could do more than one sport and also because it had winning teams. Some of his teammates in the NFL did not enjoy college as much, finding it cutthroat and a constant battle to keep their scholarships.

On the 1996 team, in addition to Hammer All-Americans Walker and Brooks, Brian Consigli was runner up in that discipline, while there were also two women Hammer All-Americans. Consigli notes, "The wonderful thing about Williams is it fosters a real competitiveness, both academically and athletically. (Walker) was the best athlete I ever played with but also one of the best human beings I know. Williams was full of people you could say that about." "By virtue of attending Williams, I always found it very competitive.

The people I met and competed against were the best of the best. They always pushed you to get a little more out of yourself. I still gain from that today, to squeeze a little bit more out of yourself. The other great thing about Williams is so many people compete in sports. So talented and well-rounded."

The 1996 men's indoor team won their 5th consecutive Division III New England crown. Derek Sasaki-Scanlon started it off with a come-from-behind last event 1000 meters in the pentathlon to take the prize. Ethan Brooks set new facility records in winning both the shot put (49'11") and weight toss (56'7 ½"). Creaghan Trainor won the 800 in 1:57.50, Marzuki Stevens the 3000 in 8:36.80, and Jeremie Perry the 5000 in 15:02.90. Tim Allsopp won the 200 in new school and meet record time of 22.40, and also anchored the runnerup 4x400 relay with a blazing 48.5 split.

At the indoor Division I New Englands, several Ephs stood out. Creaghan Trainor broke the existing 800 standard with a 1:52.13 silver medal. Ethan Brooks grabbed third in both the shot and weight throw. Tim Allsopp established a new mark in the 400 with a 48.65, good for fourth place. He also anchored the 4x400 relay, splitting a 48.1 as the quartet ran 3:18.37 to qualify for nationals.

At the women's Div I NE's, there were also several notable performances. Junior Brenda Start threw 51'10" for sixth place. Yvonne Barnes ran 2:15.85 in the 800, good for second. Amy MacDonald ran a 10:30.04 3000 for a third place PR (personal record). In addition, Meg Randall ran 18:18.5 in the 5000 for sixth.

The Indoor Nationals were held at Smith College in Northampton MA. All told, seven men and two women came back with All-American honors. Brooks led the charge with a new facility and Division III record 63' 8 ¾" toss in the weight throw. He also placed fourth in the shot put. Trainor put on a tremendous kick to win the 800 in 1:52 flat. Marzuki Stevens grabbed fourth in the 5000 at 14:37, while the 4x400 team of Clark, Woelfel, Iliff, and Allsopp placed fourth in 3:19.0. For the women Barnes earned an impressive second place in the 800 at 2:14.65, while Start was third at the weight throw with a new school record 51'11".

That spring, both men and women captured the Div. III New Englands, the men winning their sixth consecutive, the women their fifth. The men were once again led by superstar Brooks, who won both the shot put and discus, while settling for second in the hammer throw. Tim Allsopp captured the 200 in 21.87 and also anchored victorious 4x100 and 4x400 relay squads, running with Stuart Wade, Sam Young, and John Berry in the shorter run, and Konrad Davis, Matt Woelful, and Chas Iliff in the longer. Davis also captured first in the 400 hurdles, while Keith Long won the steeplechase and Paul Alsdorf and Jeremie Perry went 1-2 in the 5000. Derek Sasaki-Scanlon won the decathlon and finished fourth in the pole vault, while Marzuki Stevens (1500) and Jesse McCarron (vault) also grabbed silver medals.

At the Women's Outdoor Div III New Englands, Williams was paced by the efforts of sprinter Carrie Elson, who took top honors in both the 100 and 200, while anchoring the fifth place 4x100 and runnerup 4x400. Brenda Start took first in the hammer, third in the discus, and sixth in the javelin. Catherine Bolton captured the long jump at 17'5 ½", while the 4x800 took top spot in 9:37.99.

At the men's Division I New Englands, Williams posted an impressive second place finish. Marzuki Stephens and Keith Long went 1-2 in 9:06.04 and 9:14.02, while the 4x400 posted a second place time of 3:13.28, a new school record. Allsopp ran an exceptional 47.56 to take the 400, while Trainor was fourth in the 800 at 1:51.68. Brooks was busy as usual, with second in the discus, fourth in the hammer, and sixth in the shot put.

The Nationals were either a tremendous performance, or a terrible heartbreak, depending on perspective. The Ephs entered the final event, the 4x400, needing only a seventh place finish, but unfortunately they false started and were disqualified. Highlights included Brooks winning the hammer at 194'10", while earning second a third all-american with second in the discus at 171' even and fifth in the shot at 52'4 ¼". Stevens and Long continued their streak in the steeplechase, capturing first and second, while Trainor came from behind to cop the 800 in 1:51.10. Meanwhile, freshman Allsopp was an impressive third in the 400 at 47.61. For the women, 18th seeded Kirsten Paquette came through big time with 1:03.69 for fourth in the 400 hurdles, and Brenda Start was second in the hammer at 176'8".

Tim Billo '97 sends the following few paragraphs about the team at that time:

"Pete Farwell was a particularly talented coach I think. He had a lot of talented runners and he had a knack for keeping everyone healthy and performing to the best of their potential. The atmosphere on the team was low-key and team oriented. He was also good at allowing people who came in from strong high school programs to keep doing some of the things that worked for them in high school. In other words, while he had some very good workouts that everyone did, there was some flexibility built in. I especially liked the hill workouts, intervals on the golf course, and long Sunday runs in the mountains. For me, the beauty and wildness of the Purple valley was one of the most rewarding aspects of running at Williams. We embraced mountain running, and out team was tougher for it. I am a biologist now, and I am grateful for all of the wild areas I was able to explore around Williamstown through running (and that Pete encouraged it). I also learned about alternative workouts at Williams, namely biking and swimming. This was something Pete definitely introduced to my training repertoire.

"The track team was always a hodgepodge of people--the core group of cross country runners merged with the weight throwers and sprinters who would come on in the winter and spring. A lot of very different breeds of people, yet somehow we all managed to come together and accomplish a lot as a team. I think there was a lot of mutual respect. Our throwers were an especially tight knit group--Bobby Walker, Ethan Brooks, and Brian Consigli...And they trained hard too. There was a lot of mutual respect there--the distance runners and the throwers were always racking up points at meets. And Brent Wilson was a phenom in the 100. A quiet guy--don't know what his background was and I'm pretty sure he didn't do other sports during the rest of the year. He was unbeatable though and a really solid guy. I remember once sitting down with Ethan Brooks in the dining hall (probably 2 times my body weight) and going head to head with him in an impromptu eating match after a hard afternoon down at the track. We went back for plate after plate of food. Eating was one area where I could definitely compete with the largest throwers/football players. I still have a large appetite, but it has subsided a little since college. And I'm still more or less the same weight I was in college!

"I went to Williams because I cared about academics and running. I wanted a serious running program with serious runners in a small school atmosphere. I also liked the camaraderie of the team and wanted to be a part of it. The setting and the knowledge that I would get to do plenty of rugged trail runs sealed the deal. I have no doubt it was the right choice for running. I could have not have asked for a better experience. I turned down offers from Dartmouth and Stanford to run for Williams. I was glad we competed against Div 1 schools occasionally because I did often want to know how we measured up. We often didn't face serious competition until nationals and this was a weakness of being a great team in a fairly weak league. I was pleased to know that we could hold our own with or beat the best Div 1 teams in New England.

"The only other thing I can think of worth mentioning were some of our epic spring break trips to Florida. I still hold records on a few tracks going down the eastern seaboard. I remember pulling into Panama City for spring break with the track van surrounded by hordes of drunken college kids who thought our van and the vaulting poles on top were part of some big beach party set-up. I remember them chanting the "party van is here". Our biggest event was the Florida Relays. An incredible sprint event. The southern sprint culture was awesome and the excitement in the 4x100 was palpable as the nation's best college sprinters went head to head. The stadium was full of spectators and the place was wild. There were some incredible athletes there and I was definitely exposed to a sprint culture and ritual very unlike anything I'd seen in New England. It was perhaps more akin to the some of the high school meets I ran in DC and Virginia growing up, but this was the best of college sprinting and it was a whole new level. The distance events were just an afterthought--perhaps light entertainment--a bunch of skinny guys jogging around for light entertainment after the main events of the day were over. We ran the distance medley late at night and did OK as I remember. I think we set the school record at the time. I dislocated my shoulder subsequently in one of my first steeple chases ever, putting a damper on the end of that trip."

The next winter, 1997, the women once again won the Indoor Division III New England crown. Start led the way with a weight throw toss of 16.06 meters, a new school record. She also took fifth in the shot put. Elson captured the dash in 7.42 and the 200 in 26.22. Lisel James took second in the long jump at 5.15m and third in the hurdles at 8.68. Meg Randall '99 won the 5000 in 18:22.36, while Deb Frisone was second in 18:24.15. Amy MacDonald was first in the 3000 in 10:34.68, while Kate Dreher was third in the 1000 at 3:04.84. Finally, Catherine Bolton finished second in the pentathlon with 2,785 points.

Meanwhile the men also captured their Div III NE title. Co-captain Derek Sasaki-Scanlon got things going with a pentathlon title of 3,429 points, while finishing second in the long jump and fourth in the pole vault. Geoff Findlay won the vault at 15' even. Allsop captured the 400 in 50.51, while Dave Stuhlstaz grabbed the shot in 51'7 ¾". Brent Wilson was second in the 200 and third in the dash, while Paul Alsdorf won the 5,000 in 15:08. At the Nationals, tri-captain Brenda Start secured all-american status with a weight toss of 51'9" (15.77m), good for fourth place.

That spring, picking up right where they left off, both men and women captured the NESCAC title, as well as Division III New Englands. The women won at Middlebury College, scoring 199 to the host school's second place 124. The leaders were Kirsten Paquette and Start. Kirsten won the 400 in 58.65 as well as the 400 hurdles in 63.49. She also PR'd in the long jump for third and anchored the winning 4x400 relay. Start won both the hammer and discus with new NESCAC records while Rebecca Brooks '00 was shot put runnerup with a new school record 40'6" and placed sixth in both the javelin and discus. Carrie Elson was first in the 200 at 25.9 and second in the 100 at 12.75, while Lisel James won the long jump at 17'4 3/4". Marie Glancy and Edie DeNiro went 1-2 in the 10000, while

Deb Frisone and Amy MacDonald were 2-3 in the 5000. Meanwhile, both the 4x800 team of Trzeszkowski, Crowley, Dreher, and O'Connor (9:31.13) and the 4x400 team of Harnisch, Metzger, Elson, and Paquette (3:56.53) proved victorious.

On the men's side, their fifth consecutive NESCAC title was sparked by Tim Allsopp's meet record 47.56 in the 400, as he also anchored the first place 4x100 team of Young, Wilson and Berry to a 42.83 win and split 47.1 to anchor the 4x400 to runnerup status. Other wins came from Tim Billo in the 10000 at 31:22.74 and Dave Stuhlsatz in the shot put at 48'3". Showing versatility, Derek Sasaki-Scanlon was second in the pole vault, third in the long jump, and third in the high hurdles. Runnerup ribbons went to Brent Wilson in the 100, Brendan Burns in the steeplechase, and Ted Grannatt in the javelin.

At the Division III New Englands, the women's 144.5 more than doubled runnerup Springfield's 71.5. Deb Frisone got things started with a 37:56 10K, good for first place. Meg Randall and Ellen Roh went 1-2 in the 5K, while Amy MacDonald's 10:24 was good for second in the 3000. Rebecca Brooks won the shot in 42'8", and continued things with a winning javelin heave of 109'. Start qualified for the nationals with a 172'10" hammer toss, good for top honors, while James was second in the long jump. Finally, Elson was first in the 200 and second in the 100.

Rebecca Brooks

On the men's side, Allsopp continued his dominance with 10.74 and 21.29 victories in the 100 and 200. He also anchored victorious 4x100 and 4x400 relay teams. Sasaki-Scanlon won the decathlon with 6,443 points as well as the pole vault at 14'3" and grabbed fourth in the high hurdles. Stuhlsatz and Kurt Knuppel were second in the shot put and javelin, respectively,

In 1998, the men's team captured its seventh consecutive New England Division III indoor title by a scant two points over rival MIT. Sasaki-Scanlon won the pentathlon and was fourth in the long jump, but unfortunately suffered an injury in the latter event and was out of further competition. But Stuhlsatz won the shot at 53'11", and the team earned twenty points in the 3000 with Paul Alsdorf, Tim Campbell and Dan McCue finishing first, third and fourth. The deciding event was the 4x400, and the foursome of Rossier, Young, Alozie, and Decamp did not disappoint, with a 3:26.54 clocking, good for third place to clinch the meet.

At the Division I New Englands, Alsdorf was second in the 5000 at 14:46.24, while Stuhlsatz was third at 53'5 ½" The same duo impressed at the Nationals, with Stuhlsatz throwing 54'5 ½" for third, and Alsdorf finishing fourth in 14:35.92.

The highlight of the 1999 women's indoor campaign was provided by Marblehead MA's Tara Crowley in the 1500. First she set a new school record of 4:37, then topped that with a 4:35.39 at nationals for second place. At the NESCAC's that spring, the women continued their winning ways, with senior Jill Metzger leading the way. Jill won the 400 at 58.28, then grabbed the 400 hurdles at 64.79. But she was not done there as she ran an amazing anchor for the victorious 4x400. Crowley was second at the 1500, while Rebecca Brooks won both the hammer and shot put. First year Katie Worth grabbed the 800 in 2:14.62, while sophomore Sandra DiPillo won the 5000 and Rebecca Atkinson and Meg Randall took 3-4 in the 3000.

At the ECAC the women won their fifth title in seven years with 57 points. Randall won the 5000 at 17:44.39, while sophomore Courtney Bennigson was second in the 10000 at 37:29.21. Crowley (4:35.71) and Katie Worth (2:14.25) were second in the 1500 and 800, respectively. Brooks won the shot put and was fourth in the hammer, while first year Diane Williams was second in the hammer. The 4x400 foursome of Rearick, O'Connor, Worth, and Metzger proved victorious, while the 4x800 group of Sharff, Wiener, O'Brien and Crowley was second.

The women's outdoor records as of April 16, 1999 were as follows:

100 – 12.26 – Carrie Elson.

200 – 25.03 (w) – Elson

400 – 56.99 – Elson

100 h – 15.13 – Kira Shields

400 h – 60.76 – Dawn Macauley

800 – 2:13.26 – Katie Worth

1500 – 4:28.64 – Ann Dannhauer

3000 – 9:54.61 – Anne Platt

5000 – 17:24.42 – Ann Bokman

10000 – 35:43.65 – Bokman

4x100 – 49.96 – James, Elson, Paquette, Olmstead

4x400 – 3:54.08 – Trzeszkowski, Metzger, Paquette, Elson

4x800 – 9:10.14 – Donna, Macauley, Barndollar, Gray

Shot Put – 44'8 ¼" – Rebecca Brooks

Discus – 133'3" - Brenda Start

Javelin – 115'7" – Start

Hammer – 179'5" – Start

High Jump – 5'5 ½" – Angela Carcia

Long Jump – 17'10 ½"- Lisel James

Triple Jump – 36'2" – Susan Vaill

Pole Vault – 9'0" – Catherine Bolten, Melissa Purdy

Heptathlon – 4,128 – Cathleen Miller

Steeplechase – 12:52.41 – Erin Curtis

At the 2000 women's indoor nationals, the Lady Ephs performed in impressive fashion. First year Healy Thompson led the way with a 43'8 ½" victory in the shot put, while teammate Diane Williams chipped in for fifth. The distance medley relay team of Sharff, Doody, Worth and Crowley brought home the gold medal in 11:59.46, with Crowley returning to the track for third in the 1500 at 4:37.38. Meanwhile, first-year Rita Forte destroyed her one-week old school record in the hurdles with a time of 8.15, good for third. The team thus scored 34 points to place third in this NCAA meet.

That spring, the women returned to the top of the podium at the Division III New Englands. The throwing corps led the way, with Healy Thompson, Rebecca Brooks, and Diane Williams going 1-2-3 in the shot put. Williams would go on to cop the discus title with 45.69 meters, good for a new school record. On the track, Crowley won the 1500 in 4:36.89, while Lauren Krisko and Rebecca Atkinson went 2-3 in the 3000, both qualifying for nationals. To wrap up, the 4x100, 4x400, and 4x800 teams all took second place, to add to the winning margin.

Rebecca Brooks '00 played basketball in the winter but notes, "Williams track and field was a specifically unique experience....Some of the best coaches. Williams draws you in. That sport pushed me in ways more than soccer and basketball. I am much better off for it." Brooks is the sister of current head coach Fletcher Brooks and noticed a definite change when Fletcher came on board as assistant during her last two years at Williams. The main thing was that it was much more focused and intense. If classes did not intercede, practice could last from 1:00 – 7:00 PM. There could be 40 throws on one implement and 20 on another, along with sprints and at least an hour of lifting. A weekly, monthly, and season schedule was set up before things started that were very specific and very detailed. There was also a new emphasis on diet including fruits, vegetables, high protein, and no man-made carbohydrates before 5:00 PM. Of course, academics came first and you could always lift in the morning if afternoon classes were scheduled. Fletcher produced more informed, consistent throwers and Rebecca cites his coaching as the reason for improved, more consistent performance at the nationals. The throwers were a curious group, and would frequently do things a different way during meets to improve process, rather than focus simply on results. Rebecca also cites her teammates as a diverse group of "people that I will never forget."

Melissa Murphy '00, a teammate and close friend of Rebecca, brings a different, but no less essential, angle to the Williams track experience. Melissa recalls how supportive everyone was as they cheered the 4x400 relay, had t-shirts made, sang together and even drove to the nationals to see teammates perform. Workouts varied but those under Coach Farley were predictably insane. "You felt like you were dying." "I loved running, it was about my friendships. Three of my best friends to this day were from the track team. Running was secondary. It was a good balance. Ability to focus on more than one place. Ability to prioritize. (She) remembers the emotional side more than meets. "There were so many more aspects besides meets such as snacks the night before meets, you got close with the people you were training with." The "Pratt to Pratt" relay was a memorable fundraiser from Pratt House at Williams to Pratt Field at Amherst College at the time of the Homecoming football game. The relay was an overnight fundraiser for the team's spring break trip, and involved mostly track people since the Cross Country team was in season at the time.

Coach Farwell retained the head indoor and outdoor reins through the 2001 season, after which he decided to reduce his administrative load by shifting to assistant coach in track and field, while continuing as head coach of men's and women's cross country in the fall.

2002 – Present

The 2002 Division III NE indoor meet featured a memorable fight with an MIT squad that came in as 40 point favorites, as Ralph White became head coach. The Engineers began by taking places one through seven in the pentathlon, scoring 38 points, and putting Williams in a deep hole, later adding another 22 with first, second and fifth in the 600,. Williams fought back with a 1,2,3 sweep of the shot put, Then Malcolm Perry took second in the pole vault while teammate Dean Carvalho tied for third. Captain Jamiyl Peters won the dash while teammate Val von Arnim contributed a pivotal fourth. Wes Reutimann ruled the roost in the 5000 with 15:00.68. Then the Distance Medley Relay team of Brady, Ossinger, Blume and Winkler grabbed second, and the 4x400 relay of Farley, Jakobsche, Peters, and von Arnim took the gold and it was down to the 4x800. The team of Austin, Reilly, Hines, and Garvin posted a time of 8:03.98, while MIT ran 7:55.64 in another heat. The meet ended in a dead heat, both Williams and MIT having scored 150.5. "Anytime we ran against MIT it was something special. I never really got more excited than for those meets. I remember guys running and jumping with sprained ankles, while sick or with any other number of problems. Everyone wanted to go all out in that meet," said one Eph.

The outdoor track and field teams won div III NE titles on both sides. The men were at home in Williamstown where they topped rival MIT's 122 with 169.5 of their own, while the women traveled to Springfield to prevail with a score of 163.

Topping the shot put competition with the first four places were Dan Austin, Dave Fontes, Trey Wright, and Caleb Bliss. Richard Chau achieved an automatic National qualifier in the Hammer at 182'10", while captain Dwight Ho-Sang triple jumped 44'9" for second. Chuck Jakobsche gained second in the 400 at 48.66, and backed that up running anchor for the winning 4x400 team in 3:16.85 that also included Kevin Reilly, Jamiyl Peters, and Scott Farley. Peters and teammate Val von Arnim went 1-3 in the 100, while the same duo achieved second and fourth in the 200. Karl Remsen captured the steeplechase in 9:08.99 and Mitchell Baker's 32:17.45 was good for second in the 10000.

The women were likewise led by their throwers, with Anna Swisher, Diane Williams and Healy Thompson going one, two, three in the discus and

Jenn Campbell
National Champion Steeplechase

Thompson and Williams going 1-3 in the shot. Thompson also won the hammer with a prodigious throw of 164'8", good for third longest in the nation at the time. Meredith Jones pole vaulted 11' ½" to tie for second, while Jenn Campbell dropped down to the 1500 to take fourth. The 4x100 relay was third, while the 4x400 was second and 4x800, victorious.

On March 18, 2003, Healy Thompson was named the Female Athlete of the Year by the US Coaches Association for her first place shot put of 50'10.75" along with a runnerup throw of 58'5.25" in the weight at Nationals.

Healy Thompson '03
WOMEN'S FIELD
AWARDS AND ACCOLADES
NATIONAL SHOT PUT CHAMPION
ALL-AMERICAN

Healy and other women track athletes were beneficiaries of women's pioneers of the late 1970's and early '80's. Women's Track and Field began at Williams as a club sport in 1977, beating Amherst and Middlebury with the help of Renalda Pierce in the 100 yards. Coach Sue Hudson-Hamblin led the squad through 1981 when the team became varsity. Two of Williams' first standouts were Holly Perry who placed 2nd in the 1979 ECAC 400 with at time of 60.4 and Brenda Ellison with a 5'4" high jump. Other early 'pioneers' for the Ephs included Judi St. Hilaire in the high hurdles (16.3) and Melanie Taylor in the sprints (12.5 and 27.3)

Men's coach Dick Farley took over the reins of the women's program in 1982 and headed a combined program through 1987. But I digress.

At the 2003 Division III NE's, held at Williams own Tony Plansky track, the women

Elise Johnson
All American

scored 189 points, or 86 more than runnerup Colby. Julia Bensen set the tone early with a 36:27.96 win in the 10000, while rookie sensation Caroline Cretti won the 5000 at 16:59.09, establishing a new meet and Plansky Track record. Ann Schorling likewise set a new meet record in the steeplechase at 11:03.77. The record setting continued with Jenn Campbell's meet and track record 4:33.60 1500. Campbell returned for third in the 800 behind teammates Colleen Doody and Kali Moody. Joyia (Chadwick) Yorgey had a breakthrough meet in the heptathlon with 4,551 points, automatically qualifying for nationals. Joyia's hep marks in the high jump and long jump would have won both those open events. Thompson captured the shot put, while placing second in the hammer and fourth in the discus. Teammate Anna Swisher was third in the disc and sixth in the shot. Robbs, Johnson, Samuel and Doody would team up for a 49.04 4x100, while the 4x400 quartet of Samuel, Moody, Doody and Koene took top honors in 3:53.44.

Numerous school records fell at the Division I New England Indoor meet in the winter of 2004. Jenn Campbell started it off with a 4:54 mile, good for second place and third on the National list. The 4x400 secured a new school standard at 3:56, while the Distance Medley Relay did likewise in 11:48. Kristin Moss triple jumped 38' 4.25" for another school record. Kristin, who would become a four–time All American, felt that practices were a stress reliever but not so the meets. She says she never left a meet satisfied. At the same time, overall it was an enjoyable experience and she would do it again. She believes practices broke up time from studying and helped her set priorities and find a balance. She enjoyed working with Fletcher Brooks, calling him flexible and willing to listen to what she did and did not want to do.

At the indoor nationals, several Ephs earned All-American status. Moss high jumped 5'5.25" for seventh, Campbell's 4:41 1500 placed her fifth. The Distance Medley Relay team of Campbell, Lindemann, Moody, and Robbs placed fourth in 12:02. Triple Jumper Audrey Lumley-Sapanski placed eighth at 37'8". Meredith Jones pole vaulted 11'5.25" for fifth, while Neal Holtschulte was the lone male to score, running a 14:35 5000 for fourth place. Neal ran high school track in Ohio where his best times were 4:30 in the mile and 9:45 in the two mile. He made a huge improvement in college which he credits to being indoctrinated into the history of the team, with its spirit and tradition. Neal believes Peter Farwell is perfect for a Division III program, with the exact right balance of sports and academics. He knows a lot about running and what his athletes are going through. There were many meets where the team was not expected to win but it's very much a comeback team with an underdog mentality. Workouts were frequently a long run on Sunday, pool workout Monday, Tuesdays and Thursdays were the main days while Wednesday and Fridays were hard early in the season but tapered off later on.

Running for Neal was a release from the academic grind and the pressure in the classroom. Success on the track helped with his confidence. He still runs competitively today out of Rochester New York, usually between 5 and 15K. He reports, "I miss being part of such a strong team. We worked really hard to get to know people doing other events. Spring trips put one person from each group in each room."

Typical workouts at the time were: 1. 4x400 @ 70 second, 1 mile under 5:00, 4 x 400 at 65. 2. Mile, 800, 400, 400 at increasingly fast pace. 3. 1200 in 3:33, 18 minute tempo, 1200 @ 3:33, all out 400.

Many Ephs shined at the Division I New England indoor meet of 2005. Lissy Robie improved her 800 PR by two seconds to 2:16.6, while Katie Howard qualified for the 400 final in 58.70. Caroline Cretti won the 3000 and set a school record of 9:33.8, while the 4x400 quartet of Johnson, Howard, Plitt and Ivey blazed to a 3:54.22 clocking. Abelee Esparza improved her weight throw to 49'5.75", while the distance medley relay team of Campbell, Hanley, Moody, and Cretti ran to a new school record of 11:46.9.

Caroline Cretti
National Champion

That spring, the women would win both the NESCAC's and Div III NE's, while the men would capture their 12th Div III Ne in 14 years. The women were led by their throwing events, taking places 2-5 in the shot put with Katie Krause, Alex Philips, Anna Swisher and Anna Morrison. Then Morrison and Swisher went one-two in the discus, and Swisher also took third in the hammer. Kristin Moss placed second in both the high jump and triple jump, and third in the long jump. Caroline Doctor was second in the long jump but first in the triple. Katie Fulton continued the festivities by taking the 100 and 200 and anchoring the 4x100 to victory, passing three teams in the final stretch. Veronica Ivey ran a leg on the 4x100 and also was first in the 400, third in the 200, and second in the 4x400 along with Caitlin Hanley, Afton Johnson, and Katie Howard. Meanwhile, Kali Moody was second in the 800 and Lissy Robie PR'ed in the 1500 for second.

At the Div III NE's, the women more than doubled runner up Amherst's 82 with 198 points. Anna Morrison and Anna Swisher went one two in the discus, while Katie Krause, Swisher, and Abelee Esparza were second, third and fifth in the shot put. Doctor and Moss went one two in the triple jump, then Doctor, Joyia Chadwick, and Moss went 2,3,5 in the long jump. Moss returned to take second in the high jump. Fulton again won both the 100 and 200 in facility record time, and anchored the 4x100 that tied for first. Afton Johnson and Julie O'Donnell went one two in the 400 hurdles, while Danner Hickman grabbed second in the steeplechase. Katie Howard won the gold in the 400 at 58.6, while Caroline Cretti doubled in the 1500 and 5K, with third and second, respectively.

John Symanski
200M All American

The men won their version of Div III's by an impressive 68 points over rival MIT. Corey Levin started things off with a runnerup position in the 10K. Branden Mirach, Joe Song, and Kyle McDermott went 2, 3, 5 in the long jump, while Markus Burns was second in the high jump. Bill Ference and Mike Davitian ran gutsy races in the 1500, finishing second and third. Drew Raab was second in the 400 at 49.37, while Tyler Gray was likewise runnerup in the 800 at 1:56.42. Dan Austin dominated the discus with a throw of 188', more than 30' better than runnerup Caleb Bliss' 155', John Symanski won both the 100 (10.70) and 200 (21.05) while anchoring the 4x100 relay. Neal Holtschulte then ran away with the 5K in 15:05.

Of all the great track athletes in school history, Austin's accomplishments probably shine brightest. He set the meet record at the Nationals in the discus, and was fourth in the discus in the U.S. National Championships, including all throwers in the country. Dan attributes his success to the balance at Williams which was a really good place to live and work hard but not get obsessed. He wanted to go to Dartmouth but was not allowed to ski and do other sports there so he went to Williams where he joined the Frisbee team and taught fly fishing. He believes Fletcher knew how his body worked and let him find his own unconventional way of throwing, being a 6'6", 240 lb. thrower, while others of his peers were more muscular and not as tall.

Jenn Campbell was national champion in the Steeplechase. "The national meets are particularly vivid in my head. I usually spent most of my time with all the distance girls. At nationals, Williams always brought a bit smaller of a crew, 15-20 people and it was my opportunity to get to know the sprinters, throwers, and jumpers. Being together for three days, on the plane, at the meet, in the hotel, we always got to know each other quite well. A strong sense of community developed quickly and the support everyone provided at the meet was amazing. I always felt like I had the loudest cheering section in the race. The meet would conclude with a gathering of Williams athletes and parents at a local restaurant. It was always a fun, laughter-filled dinner and a perfect way to end the season.

On Peter Farwell, "(He) was my primary coach and he was simply amazing. He genuinely cared about every member of the team regardless of their speed. He always took the time to check in and see how we were doing not only with the workouts, but also with our academic endeavors. Even to this day, Pete and I exchange a few emails back and forth every year. He continues to keep up with my recent races and job/grad school pursuits. He even provided me with training guidance for my first half marathon. He has a vast wealth of knowledge about the sport and knows how to train his athletes hard while still keeping it fun. Under his guidance I dropped almost 1.5 minutes off my 5k time my freshman year. I had so much fun that year going for Sunday mountain runs, relay racing in the pool, and striding on the golf course, that I never realized how hard I was working and how much I was improving.

On her Williams experience, "While in college, going to track practice and meets provided me with a strict schedule around which I had to fit in my academic endeavors. This schedule actually made me more productive as I knew as soon as I got back from practice and dinner it was time to do school work for a few hours so I could fit in 8 hours of sleep and start all over again tomorrow.

"The distance crew was like my second family at Williams. I ate dinner with them every night. I lived with some of my teammates my sophomore through senior years. Any of my free time was spent just hanging out with them. I knew if I ever needed a favor I could ask any one of them. Today I still keep in touch with a bunch of them and often meet up for a run, bike ride, or just to catch up. Sometimes I am even lucky enough to pass them along the Charles River in Boston (where we promptly stop and chat for a bit forgetting we were even on a run) or see them at a local race."

Anna Swisher '05 is the current record holder in the women's discus. Anna set the record in Williamstown with a wind favoring left-handed throwers. Men's record holder Dan Austin measured the toss as he was injured at the time. She felt this was a personal highlight as she was able to set the record in front of friends and professors.

Dan Austin
National Champion

One of the reasons Anna loved her Williams experience was working with Fletcher Brooks. He did a great job with the throwers and there are many former Eph athletes now in the coaching ranks, possibly due to the influence of the college coaching staff. The staff recognized and mentored those who looked like prospective coaches. Anna believes Williams would have been an entirely different experience without track; while the school gives you writing and analysis skills, the opportunity to have a group of people to be with and to develop close friendships enabled her to be exposed to other things besides school work.

Trey Wright '03 is a three-time All-American and current record holder in both the indoor and outdoor shot put. One of his highlights was while on spring break in San Diego. It was the beginning of outdoor season and the team was still carrying a heavy work load. For breakfast one morning Trey went to a local fast food place and ordered a one pound burrito stuffed with French Fries. He then went to the track and put the shot 55' for a new PR. Not satisfied, he ate another one pound burrito for lunch and went back to the track and threw the discus another PR of 151'.

Trey agrees that Fletcher was (and is) a very dedicated coach with great attention to detail. Fletcher would frequently sleep on the couch in his office and built up a strong throwing program which included many All-Americans and school record holders. Trey learned how to budget his time well as track was practically a school year round endeavor, with prep work starting in October and in-season travel nearly every weekend.

Trey did some coaching at the Cincinnati Country Day School which he attended as a prep, and would consider more coaching in the future, probably at the prep level. He learned a lot from Fletcher and Williams and tells the story of giving a youngster a tip while watching him throw and the athlete going out to a PR by five feet that day.

Joyia (Chadwick) Yorgey '05 ended her Williams career by winning the national title in the heptathlon. Coach Brooks says he never knew a better competitor than Joyia. She knew just the right level of effort to put forth. Joyia was also an All-American in volleyball. After the fall volleyball season, Joyia generally took December off and joined the track team in January. She never hurdled or threw the javelin before college but the coaching staff felt her strength might be as a multi-eventer, so she learned them. She focused on weight training to learn the shot. She says there was not enough time in the day to master all seven events of the heptathlon (100h, high jump, shot put, 200, long jump, javelin, 800) so in keeping with the Williams experience she valued the process of learning the events which is something she applies to her whole life. "Liberal Arts teach you how to think."

One of her career highlights was Div III NE's of 2003 where she PR'd in five events and made a quantum leap forward in her event. Another was competing in the Penn Relays senior year against Division I talent where she finished fifth. "I am so thrilled that (Fletcher Brooks) is the head coach at Williams." She believes he really knows the technical aspects and has a good rapport with the athletes. She also recalls Anna Swisher as one of her best friends, "I am thankful for being on the team with her."

Mike Davitian (L) and Chris Beeler (R)
All Americans at Div III NE Championships

Joyia still works out and completed a marathon last summer. She is more involved in club volleyball and also recently played beach volleyball. She finished grad school in international politics and wants to go into non-profit policy research or urban policy issues.

In the indoor season of 2006, the Ephs impressed at Div. I New Englands, particularly in the relays. The men's distance medley started things off victoriously, with a new school record, 9:56. Bill Ference led things off with a 3:04 1200, George Rodriguez clocked 48. for the 400 leg, Chris Beeler ran the 800 in 1:53, and Mike Davitian brought the baton home with a 4:09 1600. The women kept up their side of the bargain as Lissie Robie, Veronica Ivey, Heather

Lissy Robie
All American

Bemis, and Caroline Cretti grabbed the gold medal in 11:51. Cretti's 4:53 anchor leg sealed the deal.

Tyler Gray ran the 800 in 1:52.29 for third, while Liz Gleason and Mallory Harlin went 2-3 in the 5000, both timed in 17:11. Maddie Outman posted a new school record for second place in the pentathlon with 3254 points, while Katie Fulton's 24.79 200 was another school record. The men's 4x400 of Seferis, Rodriguez, Symanski and Hoerman sped through in 3:14.05, another Williams standard good for second, while the women's team of Howard, Ivey, Outman and Plitt chopped two seconds off the Williams mark in 3:50.43, to win the event.

The 2006 women's indoor team performed nobly at the nationals, finishing second to a strong University of Wisconsin-Oshkosh squad. Kristin Moss posted a strong third place in the high jump at 5'6.5". Caroline Doctor earned All-American status with a fifth place triple jump of 37'9.5". Lissie Robie chipped in with seventh in the 800, and Caroline Cretti blew away the 5000 field to become national champion in 16:44. The distance medley relay team was fifth, while the 4x400 team of Howard, Plitt, Ivey and Bemis finished sixth to close the scoring.

Maddy Outman
All American in 4 events

The 2007 women's indoor team one-upped the previous year's to become the first ever Eph Track and Field team national champion! The eight women who traveled to Rose Hulman Institute of Technology in Terre Haute, Indiana posted the first ever women's national team championship with 42 points, to runnerup City College of New York's 35. Maddy Outman and Caroline Doctor started things out in fine fashion in the long jump with 2nd and 4th, respectively, at 18'7.75" and 18'5". Outman's jump was especially clutch and unexpected, and established a new school record. Doctor followed with a runnerup ribbon in the triple jump. The distance medley team of Robie, Heaslip, Howard, and Kondratjeva then came in fifth in 11:53. Shot putter Alex Philips put it all together to throw 45'0.5" for fourth. Kondratjeva posted sixth in the mile at 4:57.48, while the amazingly versatile Outman was fifth in both the hurdles and 400. All the team members felt the day-to-day encouragement of team members who may not have qualified for the meet was essential to the victory. The 4x400 team of Howard, Outman, Heaslip, and Bemis finished the meet with an eighth place finish.

That spring, both men and women again won Div III New Englands. Branden Mirach started things off for the men with a fine runnerup triple jump of 46'11", while Joe Song was third in the long jump, just one quarter inch shy of 23'. Chris Ellis-Ferrara and Stephen Wills went one-two in the steeplechase. Mike Davitian captured the 1500 in 3:54, while Tyler Gray and Edgar Kosgey were 2-3 in the 800. Andrew Arons and Deividas Seferis were second and third, respectively, in the 200, while Alex Hoerman took the blue ribbon in the 400 at 49.30. Hoerman, Seferis, Arons and Nick Reynolds combined to place second in the 4x100.

Maddy Outman led the women by capturing both the 100 and 400 hurdles, as well as third in the long jump. Carrie Plitt won both the 100 and 200, and teamed with Emily Heaslip, Halley Smith, and Shawna McArdle to win the

Carrie Plitt '08

4x100. Anna Morrison was second in the discus, while Doctor took the gold in the triple jump. Olga Kondratjeva was second in the 1500.

Says Halley Smith, "Why was Williams track so important to me? Williams is a place that really lives up to its motto, "Aim high, aim far, your goal the sky, your aim the star." It believes in you, wants nothing but the best for you, and accepts nothing but the best from you. Williams professors intellectually push you until you think and analyze in ways you were never able to before, never letting you get away with anything but your best. Track was the physical equivalent of that. Our coaches and teammates knew what we were capable of, and were devoted to helping us surpass that. I remember at a meet over spring break in Santa Barbara, our coach, Ralph White let us pick our seed times for a race. I gave what I thought was a pretty optimistic time, only to have one of my best friends, Veronica, immediately shoot me a look and say "Oh, come on. You can do better." So, terrifyingly enough, the time dropped, and I came closer to hitting that time than I ever would have imagined. It is too rare a thing to have people believe in you and support you like that, even if you're sometimes a hesitant participant!

"The only downside of it all was being injured, especially my senior year. I herniated a couple discs my freshman year, and managed to worsen one of them last spring, meaning I was in a little bit of pain. I remember our throws/strength coach, Matt Campanelli had to tell me I was done sprinting for the season instead of our sprint coach, I think because he knew I'd listen to him if he told me no. I wouldn't quit if my back hurt, and I couldn't get it through my thick skull that I wasn't going to perform well if I was in pain. I was such a terrible athlete; I kept trying to throw and failing by a larger and larger measure, not hitting remotely the distances I should or could have, seething because I couldn't just train harder to get there. Not a dream situation for anyone, coach, teammate, or athlete. I really regret that. It was funny, I came late to it, but shot put and Coach Camp and the other throwers really embodied all that was positive about my senior year in track. I just really didn't want to lose it all. So, I fought too hard and too stubbornly to stay in the game, never realizing that I would have been by far a better teammate and athlete if I'd just kept myself healthy."

Current Head Coach for both men's and women's indoor and outdoor programs Fletcher Brooks started as an assistant at Williams from 1998 to 2005. He then became head coach at MIT for three years before returning to Williamstown. "To work with young people putting forth that effort made me come back." Brooks gives a lot of attention to each athlete to support individual success for each. Healy Thompson had a tremendous rivalry with Liz Wanliss of Bates. Fletcher worked with Healy to disregard early season losses to Wanliss, focusing on peaking at the right time, which was the nationals. Liz won all their competitions up to that point, but Healy focused on nutrition and diet, as well as her ability to move across the circle quickly and explosively. Healy was fortunate to throw first before Wanliss and set the tone with a strong first toss. This was exactly as Brooks planned and forced the Bates girl to press as she struggled (unsuccessfully) to better Thompson. This in turn helped Healy to learn to focus better and look down the line in outdoors and believe in Fletcher's training plan.

Fletcher believes NESCAC and Division III New Englands are important but also believes Nationals can be of value: by qualifying more individuals you can involve more of the team, and certainly who would not want to win a national title?!

Alex Phillips

Women's Records

Women's Outdoor Track & Field Records

100 Meters	Katie Fulton	11.99	2004
200 Meters	Katie Fulton	24.65	2004
	Katie Fulton	24.12w	2006
400 Meters	Colleen Doody	56.70	2003
100 Meter Hurdles	Maddy Outman	14.20	2007
400 Meter Hurdles	Dawn Macauley	60.76	1989
800 Meters	Lizzy Danhakl	2:11.64	2008

1500 Meters	Jenn Campbell	4:28.64	2003
3000 Meters	Anne Platt	9:54.61	1990
3000 Meter Steeplechase	Jenn Campbell	10:30.21	2003
5000 Meters	Caroline Cretti	16:29.70	2003
10000 Meters	Caroline Cretti	34:35.71	2003
4x100 Meter Relay	Samuel, Jones, Robbs, Fulton	47.64	2004
4x200 Meter Relay	Samuel, Jones, Robbs, Fulton	1:43.57	2006
4x400 Meter Relay	Outman, Howard, Plitt, Heaslip	3:45.40	2007
4x800 Meter Relay	Bemis, Williams, Kondratjeva, Robie	9:09.67	2008
4x1600 Meter Relay	Zwiebel, Rhodes, Donna, Macauley	21:14.54	1992
Distance Medley Relay	Worth, O'Connor, Sharff, Crowley	12:06.49	1999
Shot Put	Healy Thompson	50'3.5"	2003
Discus	Anna Swisher	153'0"	2004
Javelin	Joyia Chadwick	125'9"	2005
Hammer	Brenda Start	179'5"	1997
High Jump	Joyia Chadwick	5'7"	2004
	Kristin Moss	5'7"	2006
Long Jump	Kristin Moss	19'0"	2006
Triple Jump	Caroline Doctor	40'4.75"	2007
Pole Vault	Meredith Jones	11'7.75"	2003
Heptathlon	Joyia Chadwick	4,931	2005

Women's Indoor Track & Field Records

55 Meters	Rita Forte	7.19	2001
55 Meter Hurdles	Rita Forte	7.99	2001
60 Meters	Katie Fulton	7.97	2006
200 Meters	Katie Fulton	24.79	2006
300 Meters	Katie Fulton	40.76	2006
400 Meters	Maddy Outman	56.91	2007
500 Meters	Katie Howard	1:16.30	2006
600 Meters	Katie Howard	1:35.52	2007
800 Meters	Kali Moody	2:12.75	2005
1000 Yards	Christie Dempsey	2:44.2	1989
1000 Meters	Olga Kondratjeva	2:54.34	2007

1500 Meters	Tara Crowley	4:35.39	1999
Mile	Jenn Campbell	4:54.71	2004
3000 Meters	Caroline Cretti	9:33.83	2005
5000 Meters	Caroline Cretti	16:44.57	2006
4x200 Meter Relay	Fulton, Robbs, Johnson, Samuel	1:45.56	2004
4x400 Meter Relay	Heaslip, Plitt, Outman, Howard	3:49.44	2007
4x800 Meter Relay	Clarke, Williams, Shea, Kondratjeva	9:17.35	2008
Sprint Medley Relay	Elson, Harnisch, Metzger, Barnes	4:09.3	1996
Distance Medley Relay	Campbell, Hanley, Moody, Cretti	11:46.92	2005
Shot Put	Healy Thompson	50'10.75"	2003
Weight Throw	Healy Thompson	58'5.25"	2003
High Jump	Kristin Moss	5'7"	2006
Long Jump	Maddy Outman	18'7.75"	2007
Triple Jump	Caroline Doctor	39'1.25"	2007
Pole Vault	Meredith Jones	11'11.75"	2002
Pentathlon	Maddy Outman	3,461	2007

Men's Records

Men's Outdoor Track & Field Records

100 Meters	Andrew Arons	10.68	2007
	Robert Schumo	9.7y	1939
200 Meters	Andrew Arons	21.14	2008
400 Meters	Tim Allsopp	47.01	1997
110 Meter Hurdles	Andre Burrell	14.58	1994
400 Meter Hurdles	Mike Reed	52.17y	1975
	Sal Salamone	52.16	1993
800 Meters	Andre Lopez	1:50.3	1986
1500 Meters	Macklin Chaffee	3:47.43	2008
3000 Meter Steeplechase	Marzuki Stevens	8:52.41	1996
5000 Meters	Paul Alsdorf	14:22.27	1999
10000 Meters	Neal Holtschulte	30:05.68	2004
4x100 Meter Relay	Arons, Raab, Mokgosi, Symanski	40.56	2005
4x200 Meter Relay	Clarke, Blecher, Duff, Wilson	1:28.4	1994
4x400 Meter Relay	Fitzgerald, Seferis, Nagy, Hoerman	3:13.24	2009

4x800 Meter Relay	Brickley, Chaffee, Cole, Kosgey	7:40.86	2008
4x1500 Meter Relay	Perry, Long, Li, Stevens	16:12.02	1996
Distance Medley Relay	Brady, Raab, Ference, Winkler	10:07.85	2004
Shot Put	Trey Wright	55'3.75"	2002
Discus	Dan Austin	196'11"	2006
Javelin (old)	Tom Lester	216'8"	1972
Javelin (new)	Dave DelaCruz	201'8"	1995
Hammer	Bobby Walker	196'5"	1995
High Jump	Brandt Johnson	6'10"	1985
Long Jump	Branden Mirach	23'10"	2006
Triple Jump	Jason Mirach	48'6.25"	2000
	Branden Mirach	48'6.25" w	2006
Pole Vault	Malcolm Perry	15'9"	2002
Decathlon	Derek Sasaki-Scanlon	6,781	1997

Men's Indoor Track & Field Records

55 Meters	John Symanski	6.44	2005
	Joe Newsome	6.2y	1973
	Brent Wilson	6.2	1997
55 Meter Hurdles	Mike Reed	7.3y	1975
	Andre Burrell	7.61	1994
60 Meters	Andrew Arons	6.97	2006
200 Meters	John Symanski	21.65	2005
300 Meters	Deividas Seferis	35.14	2006
400 Meters	Tim Allsopp	48.65	1996
500 Meters	Calvin Schnure	1:04.74	1981
600 Meters	Tyler Gray	1:21.15	2007
800 Meters	Creaghan Trainor	1:52.00	1996
1000 Meters	Macklin Chaffee	2:26.82	2009
1500 Meters	Matt Winkler	3:51.71	2003
Mile	Bo Parker	4:09.82	1983
3000 Meters	Marzuki Stevens	8:18.16	1995
5000 Meters	Neal Holtschulte	14:28.22	2004

Event	Athletes	Performance	Year
4x200 Meter Relay	Arons, Seferis, Szymanski, Reynolds	1:30.69	2001
4x400 Meter Relay	Seferis, Rodriguez, Symanski, Hoerman	3:14.05	2006
4x800 Meter Relay	Garvin, Reilly, Winkler, Slowik	7:42.77	2001
Sprint Medley Relay	Farley, Peters, Jakobsche, Reilly	3:29.6	2002
Distance Medley Relay	Brickley, Arons, Kosgey, Chaffee	9:53.57	2008
Shot Put	Trey Wright	55'7"	2003
Weight Throw	Ethan Brooks	63'8.75"	1995
High Jump	Todd Ducharme	6'9.75"	1993
Long Jump	Scott Perry	24'0.25"	1976
Triple Jump	Geoff Igharo	48'1.25"	1990
Pole Vault	Derek Sasaki-Scanlon	15'3"	1997
Pentathlon	Derek Sasaki-Scanlon	3,517	1996

Men's All-Americans

Year	Name	Event	Performance	Place
1975	Mike Reed	440y Int. Hurdles	52.17	2nd
1975	Mike Reed	120y High Hurdles	14.95	3rd
1977	Larry Tanner	Hammer	173'0"	5th
1978	Larry Tanner	Hammer	178'10"	3rd
1981	Scott Mayfield	Pole Vault	14'6"	6th
1983	Tomas Alejandro	200 Meters	21.89	7th
1985	Brandt Johnson	High Jump	6'10"	4th
1986	Brandt Johnson	High Jump	6'10"	5th
1986	John Ellison	Steeplechase	9:04.4	8th
1987	Brandt Johnson	High Jump	6'8"	7th
1987	Andre Lopez	800 Meters	1:51.0	3rd
1989	Geoff Igharo	Triple Jump	47'3.75"	5th (In)
1989	Joe McGinn	Weight Throw	52'1.25"	5th (In)
1990	Geoff Igharo	Triple Jump	48'1.25"	6th (In)
1990	Marc Beitz	Steeplechase	9:09.8	4th
1991	Marc Beitz	Steeplechase	9:00.6	2nd
1991	Larry Smith, Jr.	400 Meters	48.43	6th

Year	Name	Event	Mark	Place
1992	Larry Smith, Jr.	400 Meters	47.76	4th
1992	Sal Salamone	400 Int. Hurdles	52.92	4th
1993	Seth McClennen	Steeplechase	9:04.0	4th
1993	Keith Long	Steeplechase	9:07.6	8th
1994	Chad Kurtz	1500 Meters	3:53.2	2nd
1994	Brian Consigli	Hammer	179'4"	4th
1994	Bobby Walker, Jr.	Hammer	177'5"	6th
1994	Bobby Walker, Jr.	Weight Throw	57'9"	3rd (In)
1994	Andre Burrell	110 High Hurdles	14.84	7th
1994	Clarke, Blecher, Iliff, Duff	4x400 Relay	3:22.2	5th (In)
1994	Todd Ducharme	Decathlon	6,439	7th
1994	Brent Wilson	200 Meters	21.99	8th
1995	Bobby Walker, Jr.	Weight Throw	61'1.5"	1st (In)
1995	Ethan Brooks	Weight Throw	54'10.75"	5th (In)
1995	Creaghan Trainor	800 Meters	1:53.6	3rd (In)
1995	Creaghan Trainor	800 Meters	1:52.0	2nd
1995	Creaghan Trainor	1500 Meters	3:59.1	4th
1995	Bobby Walker, Jr.	Hammer	196'5"	1st
1995	Brian Consigli	Hammer	184'1"	2nd
1995	Ethan Brooks	Hammer	174'1"	6th
1995	Ethan Brooks	Discus	160'4"	2nd
1995	Jeremie Perry	5000 Meters	14:34.1	2nd
1995	Keith Long	Steeplechase	9:16.4	8th
1995	Marzuki Stevens	Steeplechase	9:04.4	1st
1996	Marzuki Stevens	5000 Meters	14:38.0	4th (In)
1996	Ethan Brooks	Weight Throw	63'8.75"	1st (In)
1996	Ethan Brooks	Shot Put	52'3"	4th (In)
1996	Creaghan Trainor	800 Meters	1:52.0	1st (In)

Year	Athlete(s)	Event	Mark	Place
1996	Clarke, Woelfel, Iliff, Trainor	4x400 Relay	3:19.0	4th (In)
1996	Young, Wade, Berry, Allsopp	4x100 Relay	42.04	8th
1996	Tim Allsopp	400 Meters	47.61	3rd
1996	Derek Sasaki-Scanlon	Decathlon	6,546	7th
1996	Keith Long	Steeplechase	9:02.2	2nd
1996	Marzuki Stevens	Steeplechase	9:01.6	1st
1996	Creaghan Trainor	800 Meters	1:51.1	1st
1996	Ethan Brooks	Hammer	194'2"	1st
1996	Ethan Brooks	Discus	171'0"	2nd
1996	Ethan Brooks	Shot Put	52'5.25"	5th
1997	Tim Allsopp	200 Meters	21.1	2nd
1997	Tim Allsopp	400 Meters	47.38	2nd
1997	Derek Sasaki-Scanlon	Decathlon	6,781	4th
1997	Tim Billo	5000m	14:52.1	5th
1998	Paul Alsdorf	5000 Meters	14:35.9	4th (In)
1998	Dave Stuhlsatz	Shot Put	54'5.5"	3rd (In)
1998	Dave Stuhlsatz	Shot Put	53'1.75"	7th
1999	Dave Stuhlsatz	Shot Put	54'0"	6th (In)
1999	Paul Alsdorf	5000 Meters	14:58.8	5th (In)
1999	Paul Alsdorf	5000 Meters	14:39.1	6th
1999	Dave Stuhlsatz	Shot Put	54'6"	7th
1999	Tim Campbell	Steeplechase	9:02.3	2nd
2000	Matt Campanelli	Hammer	178'10"	6th
2001	Farley, Rossier, Jakobsche, Sheehan	4x400 Relay	3:23.68	6th (In)
2001	Jason Mirach	Triple Jump	48'4.5"	7th
2001	Dusty Lopez	10000 Meters	30:41.9	2nd
2001	Dusty Lopez	5000 Meters	14:57.4	4th
2001	Karl Remsen	Steeplechase	9:08.5	6th
2001	Scott Farley	400 Int. Hurdles	52.65	3rd
2002	Trey Wright	Shot Put	53'8.25"	5th (In)

Year	Name	Event	Mark	Place
2002	Trey Wright	Shot Put	51'8.25"	7th
2002	Richard Chau	Hammer	179'0"	7th
2002	Dan Austin	Discus	171'11"	2nd
2002	Karl Remsen	Steeplechase	9:06.6	4th
2003	Chris Garvin	800 Meters	1:54.9	4th (In)
2003	Matt Winkler	1500 Meters	3:51.7	3rd (In)
2003	Matt Winkler	1500 Meters	3:49.0	5th
2003	Karl Remsen	Steeplechase	8:56.5	3rd
2003	Trey Wright	Shot Put	54'1.25"	7th
2004	Neal Holtschulte	5000 Meters	14:35.3	4th (In)
2005	John Symanski	200 Meters	21.45	5th
2005	Neal Holtschulte	5000 Meters	14:48.7	7th
2005	Dan Austin	Discus	196'1"	1st
2006	Dan Austin	Weight Throw		8th (In)
2006	Chris Beeler	800 Meters	2:00.00	8th (In)
2006	Tyler Gray	800 Meters	1:57.84	7th (In)
2006	Neal Holtschulte	5000 Meters	14:48.88	8th (In)
2006	Ference, Rodriguez, Beeler, Davitian	Distance Medley Relay	10:14.07	7th (In)
2006	Andrew Arons	200 Meters	21.59w	6th
2006	Dan Austin	Shot Put	54'6.75"	6th
2006	Dan Austin	Discus Throw	195'0"	1st
2006	Dan Austin	Hammer Throw	179'5"	7th
2006	Mike Davitian	1500 Meters	3:50.95	3rd
2006	Neal Holtschulte	5000 Meters	14:57.39	5th
2006	Branden Mirach	Triple Jump	48'0.25"w	4th
2006	Branden Mirach	Long Jump	23'4"w	8th
2007	Ference, Arons, Brickley, Chaffee	Distance Medley Relay	10:07.46	8th (In)
2007	Seferis, Hoerman, Gray, Arons	4x400 Meter Relay	3:19.95	7th

Year	Name	Event	Performance	Place
2007	Chris Beeler	800 Meters	1:54.02	3rd (In)
2007	Branden Mirach	Triple Jump	47'7.25"	5th (In)
2007	David DeVaughn	Discus Throw	153'10"	6th
2007	Mike Davitian	1500 Meters	3:56.24	7th
2008	Brickley, Arons, Kosgey, Chaffee	Distance Medley Relay	10:03.06	3rd (In)
2008	Macklin Chaffee	Mile	4:15.40	8th (In)
2008	Arons, Seferis, Fitzgerald, Hoerman	4x400 Meter Relay	3:13.52	4th
2008	Andrew Arons	200 Meters	21.40	3rd
2008	Macklin Chaffee	1500 Meters	3:47.43	2nd

Women's All-Americans

Year	Name	Event	Performance	Place
1986	Dawn Macauley	400 Low Hurdles	63.24	6th
1987	Dawn Macauley	400 Low Hurdles	61.92	3rd
1988	Dawn Macauley	400 Low Hurdles	61.91	4th
1988	Ann Dannhauer	1500 Meters	4:28.6	1st
1989	Anne Platt	1500 Meters	4:42.5	6th (In)
1989	Anne Platt	3000 Meters	10:06.4	7th
1989	Ann Dannhauer	1500 Meters	4:38.7	4th
1989	Hilary Cairns	10000 Meters	37:31.7	8th
1989	Dawn Macauley	400 Low Hurdles	60.76	2nd
1990	Anne Platt	3000 Meters	9:56.1	2nd
1990	Ann Dannhauer	1500 Meters	4:33.5	5th
1990	Ann Bokman	5000 Meters	17:26.3	7th
1990	Ann Bokman	10000 Meters	35:43.6	6th
1991	Rebecca Adams	5000 Meters	17:54.1	8th
1991	Kira Shields	400 Low Hurdles	62.19	3rd
1991	Kira Shields	100 High Hurdles	15.44	7th
1992	Cherie Macauley	1500 Meters	4:42.2	7th

Year	Name	Event	Mark	Place
1992	Susan Donna	800 Meters	2:14.7	7th
1992	Lee Kiechel	400 Low Hurdles	69.8	8th
1993	Angela Carcia	High Jump	5'5.5"	4th (In)
1993	Nancy Byrne	1500 Meters	4:43.0	6th (In)
1993	Lee Kiechel	400 Low Hurdles	62.1	2nd
1993	Cathleen Miller	Heptathlon	4,086	7th
1994	Yvonne Barnes	800 Meters	2:14.0	5th
1995	Yvonne Barnes	800 Meters	2:15.3	7th
1995	Jessica Racusin	5000 Meters	17:48.1	8th
1995	Jessica Racusin	10000 Meters	36:27.6	3rd
1995	Brenda Start	Hammer	164'8"	3rd
1995	Lisa Chadderdon	Hammer	153'10"	7th
1995	Elson, Trzeszkowski, Paquette, Barnes	4x400 Relay	3:57.4	5th
1996	Yvonne Barnes	800 Meters	2:14.7	2nd (In)
1996	Brenda Start	Weight Throw	51'11"	3rd (In)
1996	Brenda Start	Hammer	176'8"	2nd
1996	Kirsten Paquette	400 Low Hurdles	63.39	4th
1996	Meg Randall	5000 Meters	18:00.68	7th
1997	Brenda Start	Weight Throw	51'9"	4th (In)
1997	Brenda Start	Hammer	169'5"	2nd
1997	Meg Randall	5000 Meters	17:38.48	5th
1997	Kirsten Paquette	400 Low Hurdles	61.84	6th
1999	Meg Randall	5000 Meters	17:53.81	6th (In)
1999	Tara Crowley	1500 Meters	4:35.4	2nd (In)
1999	Katie Worth	800 Meters	2:15.6	4th (In)
1999	Rebecca Brooks	Shot Put	44'9"	4th
2000	Sharff, Doody, Worthy, Crowley	Distance Medley Relay	11:59.5	1st (In)

Year	Athlete	Event	Mark	Place
2000	Tara Crowley	1500 Meters	4:37.4	3rd (In)
2000	Rita Forte	55 High Hurdles	8.15	3rd (In)
2000	Diane Williams	Shot Put	43'0.25"	5th (In)
2000	Healy Thompson	Shot Put	43'8.5"	1st (In)
2000	Healy Thompson	Shot Put	46'10.75"	2nd
2000	Diane Williams	Shot Put	43'0.25"	8th
2000	Rebecca Brooks	Shot Put	47'7.25"	1st
2000	Rebecca Brooks	Hammer	157'6"	8th
2000	Tara Crowley	1500 Meters	4:32.3	3rd
2001	Healy Thompson	Shot Put	44'9.75"	2nd (In)
2001	Healy Thompson	Weight Throw	57'0"	2nd (In)
2001	Rita Forte	55 Meters	7.19	5th (In)
2001	Rita Forte	55 High Hurdles	7.99	2nd (In)
2001	Rita Forte	Long Jump	17'11.5"	8th
2001	Rita Forte	100 High Hurdles	14.48	2nd
2001	Diane Williams	Shot Put	44'9.75"	2nd
2001	Diane Williams	Discus	143'0"	8th
2001	Julia Bensen	10000 Meters	36:39.5	7th
2001	Healy Thompson	Shot Put	48'7.25"	1st
2001	Healy Thompson	Hammer	161'2"	2nd
2002	Healy Thompson	Shot Put	47'4.25"	1st (In)
2002	Healy Thompson	Weight Throw	55'8.25"	3rd
2002	Diane Williams	Shot Put	44'5.5"	6th (In)
2002	Moody, Samuel, Doody, Campbell	Distance Medley Relay	12:03.5	4th
2002	Jenn Campbell	1500 Meters	4:38.4	4th (In)
2002	Jenn Campbell	Steeplechase	10:43.7	2nd

Year	Athlete	Event	Mark	Place
2002	Janna Rearick	800 Meters	2:12.0	3rd
2002	Colleen Doody	800 Meters	2:12.3	3rd
2002	Doody, Samuel, Heinrichs, Rearick	4x400 Relay	3:48.3	5th
2002	Diane Williams	Discus	144'4"	7th
2002	Healy Thompson	Shot Put	48'0.75"	2nd
2002	Healy Thompson	Hammer	165'4"	4th
2002	Torrey Baldwin	Hammer	168'4"	3rd
2002	Meredith Jones	Pole Vault	11'6.5"	7th
2003	Meredith Jones	Pole Vault	11'5"	6th (In)
2003	Kristin Moss	High Jump	5'5.25"	8th (In)
2003	Colleen Doody	800 Meters	2:17.2	8th (In)
2003	Healy Thompson	Weight Throw	58'5.25"	2nd (In)
2003	Healy Thompson	Shot Put	50'10.75"	1st (In)
2003	Jenn Campbell	1500 Meters	4:35.8	3rd (In)
2003	Schorling, Johnston, Moody, Campbell	Distance Medley Relay	11:54.1	4th
2003	Julia Bensen	5000 Meters	17:22.2	8th (In)
2003	Caroline Cretti	5000 Meters	16:55.1	3rd (In)
2003	Healy Thompson	Shot Put	49'0.75"	1st
2003	Healy Thompson	Hammer	167'4"	7th
2003	Caroline Cretti	5000 Meters	16:51.6	7th
2003	Caroline Cretti	10000 Meters	34:35.7	4th
2003	Jenn Campbell	Steeplechase	10:33.7	1st
2004	Jenn Campbell	1500 Meters	4:42.0	5th (In)
2004	Lindenman, Robbs, Moody, Campbell	Distance Medley Relay	12:03.0	4th (In)
2004	Meredith Jones	Pole Vault	11'5.25"	5th (In)

Year	Name	Event	Mark	Place
2004	Kristin Moss	High Jump	5'5.25"	7th (In)
2004	Audrey Lumley-Sap	Triple Jump	37'8"	8th (In)
2005	Caroline Cretti	5000 Meters	17:14.7	2nd (In)
2005	Caroline Cretti	10000 Meters	35:09.3	2nd
2005	Caroline Doctor	Triple Jump	38'1.25"	6th (In)
2005	Caroline Doctor	Triple Jump	39'2.5"	4th
2005	Kali Moody	800 Meters	2:15.7	6th (In)
2005	Anna Morrison	Discus	144'4"	3rd
2005	Joyia Chadwick	Heptathlon	4,931	1st
2005	Moody, Howard, Ivey, Plitt	4x400 Relay	3:55.0	5th (In)
2005	Campbell, Hanley, Moody, Cretti	Distance Medley Relay	11:57.6	3rd (In)
2006	Caroline Cretti	5000 Meters	16:44.57	1st (In)
2006	Caroline Doctor	Triple Jump		5th(In)
2006	Liz Gleason	5000 Meters	17:09.76	3rd (In)
2006	Mallory Harlin	5000 Meters	17:15.52	6th (In)
2006	Robie, Fulton, Howard, Cretti	Distance Medley Relay	12:00.85	5th (In)
2006	Kristen Moss	High Jump	5'6.5"	3rd (In)
2006	Caroline Cretti	5000 Meters	17:12.32	1st
2006	Caroline Cretti	10000 Meters	35:10.42	1st
2006	Caroline Doctor	Triple Jump	38'8.25"w	5th
2006	Caroline Doctor	Long Jump	18'6.5"w	6th
2006	Katie Fulton	200 Meters	24.12w	4th
2006	Liz Gleason	5000 Meters	17:39.24	8th
2006	Liz Gleason	10000 Meters	36:32.41	8th
2006	Kristen Moss	High Jump	5'7"	2nd
2006	Outman, Ivey, Howard, Plitt	4x400	3:53.29	8th

Year	Athlete	Event	Mark	Place
2007	Alex Phillips	Shot Put	45'0.5"	4th (In)
2007	Maddie Outman	Long Jump	18'7.75"	2nd (In)
2007	Caroline Doctor	Long Jump	18'5"	4th (In)
2007	Caroline Doctor	Triple Jump	38'9.75"	2nd (In)
2007	Robie, Heaslip, Howard, Kondratjeva	Distance Medley Relay	11:53.38	5th (In)
2007	Howard, Outman, Heaslip, Plitt	4x400 Meter Relay	3:56.24	8th (In)
2007	Maddie Outman	55 Meter Hurdles	8.29	5th (In)
2007	Olga Kondratjeva	Mile	4:57.48	6th (In)
2007	Maddie Outman	400 Meters	57.66	5th (In)
2007	Alex Phillips	Shot Put	44'9.5"	4th
2007	Caroline Doctor	Triple Jump	39'10"	2nd
2007	Outman, Howard, Plitt, Heaslip	4x400 Meter Relay	3:45.40	2nd
2007	Olga Kondratjeva	1500 Meters	4:30.39	5th
2008	Scofield, Plitt, Walls, Kondratjeva	Distance Medley Relay	11:56.56	3rd (In)
2008	Plitt, Wild, Ivey, Heaslip	4x400 Meter Relay	3:55.53	5th (In)
2008	Sara Wild	800 Meters	2:15.24	4th (In)
2008	Elise Johnson	100 Meter Hurdles	14.27w	6th

I wish to thank the following people for all their assistance in creating this book, in no particular order. Greg Crowther, Bob Kane, Peter Farwell, Jeff Garland, Melissa Murphy, Anna Swisher, Dick Farley, Fletcher Brooks, Trey Wright, Rebecca Brooks, Jay Haug, Derek Catsam, Suzanne Geer, Neal Holtschulte, Kevin Delany, Seth McClennen, Tom Cleaver, Calvin Schnure, Steve Bellerose, Lionel Bolin, Jenn Campbell, Halley Smith, Brian Consigli, Kristin Moss, Joyia (Chadwick) Yorgey, Dick Quinn, Linda Hall, Brooks Foehl, Diana Davis, Shamus Brady, and Mitchell Baker. I especially wish to thank Bill Soares for formatting the book and photos as well as editing and other services. Bill kept his word to complete the book even though he began a new job during the process, with all the stresses and commitments that involves. I apologize in advance if anyone was omitted. Special thanks to Pete Farwell for his editing assistance.

"Udderly" Ridiculous Homecoming Relay

Bibliography

Williams College Archives, 96 School Street, Williamstown MA

Credit for the following photographs to, "Williams College Archives and Special Collections, Williamstown, Mass., USA."

P. 4 – Tony Plansky

p. 5 – Outdoor Board Track

p. 6 – Williams Track and Field Records – 1950's

p. 7 – Indoor track at Williams

p. 9 – '73 Indoor Team

p. 11 - Lee Jackson

p. 12 – '79 Indoor

p. 13 – Dick Farley

p. 15 – Peter Farwell

p. 32 – Rebecca Brooks

p. 39 – Jenn Campbell

p. 40 – Healy Thompson

p. 41 – Elise Johnson

p. 43 – Caroline Cretti

p. 47 – Dan Austin

p. 49 – Mike Davitian and Chris Beeler

p. 49 – Lissy Robie

p. 50 – Maddy Outman

p. 51 – Carrie Plitt

p. 54 – Alex Phillips –courtesy Mack Brickley

p. 69 – Cow Relay – courtesy Anna Swisher

Back Cover – Athletes in Pool and also Runners at Mt. Hope – courtesy Diana Davis

www.ingramcontent.com/pod-product-compliance
Lightning Source LLC
Chambersburg PA
CBHW080526110426
42742CB00017B/3246